The Little Book of Big Motivation

The
Little Book
of
B I G
MOTIVATION

180 Simple Ways to
Overcome Obstacles and
Realize Your Goals

Eric Jensen

FAWCETT COLUMBINE / NEW YORK

A Fawcett Columbine Book
Published by Ballantine Books
Copyright © 1994 by Eric Jensen

All rights reserved under International and Pan-American Copyright Conventions. Published in the United States by Ballantine Books, a division of Random House, Inc., New York, and simultaneously in Canada by Random House of Canada Limited, Toronto.

Library of Congress Catalog Card Number: 94-94575
ISBN: 0-449-90946-8

Cover design by Kathleen Lynch
Text design by Mary A. Wirth

Manufactured in the United States of America
First Edition: January 1995
10 9 8 7 6 5 4 3 2 1

Preface

There is authentic genius inside of you just waiting to be called forth into expression. Motivation is the spark, the fire, and the passion needed to fuel that genius. Motivation handles the simplest of routines and pushes us through the most awkward and difficult of moments. It can bring us to the doorstep of destiny with an invitation to our greatest dreams. No matter how small or how big, realizing dreams is the noblest work of humanity. We ought to take our assignment seriously. Our collective future depends on it, and certainly your own future does.

Acknowledgments

My acknowledgments go to:
Richard Bandler, Ingalil-Bonet, Steven Covey, Wayne Dwyer, Martin Ford, David Gordon, Delorese Gregoire, Susan Hayward, Napoleon Hill, John-Roger, Alfie Kohn, Maxwell Maltz, Steve Snyder, Anthony Robbins, Raymond Wlodkowski, Michael Wall, and Gerald Wolfe. I appreciate the support from my assistant, Andrea Simpson, and my wife, Diane, who gives me far more than can be measured.

Introduction

Successful people are not necessarily wealthier or healthier. They do not necessarily have more education or more friends (although these certainly can help!). Successful people lead richer, more fulfilling lives by doing what is truly important and meaningful to them. In other words, they live their dreams. But doing that often requires strong motivation. Naturally, the more difficult or distasteful tasks require much more motivation than the fun ones. Yet for whatever the reason, successful people know how to get themselves to do what they have to do in order to succeed. In short, they know precisely how to motivate themselves. And successful people can (and do) do it just about any time they want.

This book is a reminder of the things that get us all motivated, and puts a wellspring right at our fingertips. I purposely included ideas from all different walks of life, social theories, learning styles, and cultural backgrounds. As a result, you'll find that some of the ideas are conflicting and contradictory. But I trust that you'll sort them all out in your own unique way and use the ones that you know will work for you. Enjoy the journey . . . *and* the destination. It was meant to be that way!

1. **Surround yourself with friends who "think positive."** We are all susceptible to the beliefs, values, and attitudes of our peers. If others around you are not motivated or are only stumbling toward an uncertain future, it will adversely affect you and your performance. It's important that you spend more time with those who are especially optimistic and motivated.

2. **Learn from your mistakes.**
Realize that all things of value, great or small, were created from accumulated wisdom. To get that wisdom, one must have experiences. And some of those experiences have to be failures—which make you stronger and smarter for the next time. Mistakes are useful ... *if* you learn from them. Have this attitude and you'll never be ashamed to try.

3. **Give yourself an extra month each year to reach your goals.** To get it, simply eliminate the false tyrannical mindset of "not enough time." Get up an extra half-hour early, or go to bed a half-hour later each night. (When you exercise better, eat better, and have positive reinforcing thoughts, you may find you *can* do with a half-hour less sleep!) Use that time to either work on your goal or on yourself. It may not be much time in and of itself, but it sure adds up. A half-hour extra, six days a week, is three hours a week. That's 166 extra hours or more than four forty-hour work weeks *extra* per year!

4. **Take one small step right now.**
"Poco a poco, se va a lejos." Little by little,
one goes far. A journey of a thousand
miles begins with a single step. To get
it done, simply start now, taking one step
at a time.

5. Troubleshoot your task.

Analyze up front any potential blocks, hazards, or uncertainties. What possible negative factors will arise? Lack of support, technical knowledge, time, physical space, energy, money, or experience can all make a task seem daunting. *Handle as many of these obstacles as early as possible.* Then you will feel much more positive about your chances for success and you will dive into the task at hand.

6. **Always create a "Plan B."** Even if you totally expect to succeed, have a back-up plan. What will you do if things don't fall into place? If others don't come through? If you get sick? If the weather becomes horrible? With an alternate plan you can relax in the knowledge that even in the worst case you'll be all right.

7. **Become an animal.** Choose a particular animal whose stereotypical temperament would help you in succeeding at your task. Consider an eagle, lion, monkey, jaguar, dolphin, shark, panther, bear, dinosaur, kangaroo, or squirrel. Make some kind of a corresponding noise, wear a hat or an article of clothing that reminds you of your chosen creature, or adopt its posture. Make it fun. Then take on your animal's temperament and start the project that is before you.

8. **Set goals that move and inspire you.** There are no unmotivated people, only unchallenging goals. Make your goals believable and exciting— and make sure that they challenge you without discouraging you. Set goals for health and vitality, and for improving relationships and character. Lackluster goals will remain on the shelf like a bad book. But powerful goals will ignite your hottest fires so that you get them done . . . now!

9. **Attach positive values to each of your tasks.** If you have to clean up the kitchen, realize that the accomplishment of the project will make you feel good about where you live. If you have to write a business proposal, associate it with making more money and gaining financial security. If you have to call a friend to discuss an uncomfortable situation, think of the call as a means of gaining courage, reducing stress, and building greater trust.

10. **Ensure that your innermost beliefs support, enhance, and further your goals.** What *do* you believe about yourself and your chances of reaching your goals? Do you believe that you *can* reach them? Will it be easy or hard? Can you do it alone or will you need help? Will reaching your goal be good for you or not? Beliefs are a key part of your ability to reach your goals. Pause now, and re-affirm your belief in yourself. Take that sense of security and confidence and start again. This will enable you to successfully accomplish any job you set before yourself.

11. **Embark on a "passion walk."** Go outside into the fresh air—the physical movement is important—and think about whatever goal is important at the moment. Walk briskly as you start vividly imagining what it would be like to accomplish that dream. It is much easier to "act" your way into feeling motivated—to *pretend* that you are—than to actually get yourself *to* act. Imagine first, and let the passion that it inspires stimulate you into doing the required task.

12. **Get public acknowledgment for completing your task.** I've developed a contact at my local newspaper. When I do something valuable that's in the public interest, I call her. Already she's done three stories on me and my accomplishments. Just thinking about getting in the paper energizes me. And putting the resulting article up on the wall keeps me inspired.

13. **Reach your goal with self-hypnosis.** Sit comfortably in an upright position, close your eyes, and relax. Breathe slowly and rhythmically for one minute. Then give yourself brief, encouraging, and clear messages of success related to your goal, such as, "I am finding my work easier and more enjoyable every day," or, "I am confident, healthy, and committed to success." Repeat your goals two or three times, either saying them out loud or to yourself. Be aware of your surroundings, yet be focused on the images, sounds, and feelings of success. Conclude your session by slowly counting down from ten to one. Tell yourself that you will feel relaxed and motivated upon reaching the number "one." Now act to achieve your goal.

14. Write down good ideas *the moment you think of them*. Keep a notepad and pen in your pocket or purse. Jot down any good ideas about how to do something better, easier, or faster. We all get good ideas, but only a few of us save them and follow through. That's often the difference between failure and success.

15. **Know your own personal habits and needs before starting a project or assignment.** Figure out if your habits will even allow you to start the job, what kind of quality they'd let you produce, and if they'd allow you to finish the project. I like being with my wife and also being near the ocean, so any task that takes me away from both for a long period of time loses my interest (unless it fulfills other important values). The same probably holds true for you, although different things may drive you: your children, the mountains, your friends. If the circumstances surrounding the task aren't the way you want them to be, stop and figure out a better way so that it will eventually be a win-win for you.

16. **Challenge yourself to do more by making an outrageous numerical prediction.** For example, if you need five possible solutions to a problem, make it your goal to brainstorm *twenty* ideas. This way, the first five will end up being easy!

17. **Keep a journal.** Personal reflection and self-initiated feedback can boost motivation, so write down your feelings, concerns, dreams, progress, and private thoughts. Review your diary often and you'll gain an appreciation for your progress and your self. But always remember "Honor Bright": *tell the truth* about your dreams and your progress on those dreams. Abiding by this saying will keep you on the right path.

18. **Keep your standards *flexible*.** If you set a particularly high standard and find it extremely difficult to achieve, change it. For example, a student who has a goal of getting an "A" in a course might find, after a month, that this goal is unattainable. Then it makes perfect sense for him or her to switch to a new, but still challenging, goal, such as getting a "B."

19. **Listen to positive audio tapes.** Some of the most motivating people are easily accessible to you every day in your car or at home on tape. Select tapes from the best motivators in the field, such as Anthony Robbins, Steven Covey, Dennis Waitley, and Zig Ziglar. Ask your friends who they think is especially stimulating, and get tapes of those people too. Then sample one, and decide for yourself.

20. **Be enthusiastic about the littlest things.** Get excited about sunshine, inspired about rain, ecstatic about snow. Be bubbly about your children's smallest deeds, in awe of a night full of stars, delighted about an opportune parking place. Then allow this childlike, joyful attitude to carry over to any task about which you'd like to be motivated. You'll be surprised at how much you'll end up accomplishing!

21. **Find out if feeling guilty works for you.** Think of how guilty, how badly you'd feel if you didn't reach your goals. You'd be letting yourself and others down. Let that awful feeling inspire you: you want to get rid of it, and the only way you *can* do that is by achieving your goals!

22. **Program your brain to succeed.** Every time you get a break or pause in your work day, think about your goal. Right before falling asleep, repeat it to yourself several times. Think about it, picture it, talk about it in your mind, make it real in your imagination. This encourages your brain to turn your goal into a fruitful obsession. Make your goals so much a part of you that they're in your subconscious, and you'll start working—however subtly—toward them.

23. **Sharpen up your self-concept.** Realize that, already, you are always motivated. You already do many times a day what *you would rather do* than *what you'd rather not*. You make dozens of choices to do *this* rather than *that*, to say *this* but not *that*, to go *here* rather than *there*. Your actions demonstrate that you already *are* motivated to do many things. Now that you have recognized that you are already motivated, your only task is to transfer some of the energy that you have given to other tasks to the one at hand.

24. **Vary the time of day at which you perform your tasks.** Our motivation levels change during the day. Morning people are best from 5 A.M. to 12 noon, others from 4 P.M. to 2 A.M. If your concentration lags, change when you do your tasks; do them at a different time until you discover your optimal energy time during the day or night. Your productivity will definitely increase as a result.

25. Squash the "good-old-days" bug. The attitude of "The best of times are all behind us" is demoralizing. When you catch yourself, a friend, or your spouse living in the past, make it a point to stop and think of something you like and appreciate about *today*. Or, think of something you are looking forward to, and get fired up about it. Also think of how you are free to do *other* things you enjoy once you get your task or goal done.

26. Advertise your successes.

Compile an inspiring collage or montage. Mount your most important goals, dreams, and projects on a poster by drawing or cutting out pictures from magazines. Now post the completed image in a conspicuous place—the wall of your office or den, refrigerator, bathroom mirror, dashboard of your car, or in your personal organizer. Then, be sure to look at the pictures every day to reinforce your need to succeed at your goals. Doing this can be very motivating!

27. **Bribe yourself.** Think of one food, reward activity, or gift that you will purposely withhold from yourself unless you achieve your aspirations. Use that as incentive to do what has to be done. *Note*: Once you reach your goal, be careful not to skimp; reward yourself with the promised treat!

28. **Get inspired by standing on a mountain—real or imagined.** Find the top of the largest hill or mountain near you and stand on it as you contemplate your goal. If there's no mountain to climb, stand on top of a chair or on a rooftop. As long as the place gives you some kind of a view and is inspiring, it'll work. Simply stand there and focus on your goal. Talk to yourself about it. Feel the inspiration and allow yourself to become even more determined to succeed.

29. **Become a "gripe-master."**
Learn to do what you need to do without
sniveling, or indulging in self-pity. The
world has little concern for your aches,
pains, and inconveniences. Meet the
world on its terms, with all its chaos,
insanity, complexity, and beauty. Rise
above your petty concerns and embrace
the world with grace and joy. Why? The
alternative to doing it this way is dreadful
to contemplate!

30. Read about someone who failed many times before succeeding, like Thomas Edison or Colonel Sanders. Or about someone who overcame tremendous hardship, like Wilma Rudolph, Captain Gerald Coffee, Jackie Joyner-Kersey, Victor Frankl, Helen Keller, Stephen Hawking, or Roger Bannister. Then ask yourself what advantages you have that they didn't. (You have many!) Now take those advantages with you, and go to work.

31. **Break it down.** If your task is overwhelming, break it down into smaller tasks that are less daunting. Think of your project as a group of chunks instead of one huge one. The reverse can also be true: if the task has too many steps—say, forty-two—turn it into seven steps of six. Then, work on just one chunk at a time. How do you eat an elephant? Well, who cares? No one eats elephants! But how do you eat over eight tons of food in a lifetime? (Most of us actually do this.) Easy: do it one bite at a time!

32. **Re-define the task to be accomplished.** Making a sales call could be viewed in any one of these "re-frames": as 1) sharing news with your soon-to-be-friends; 2) an opportunity to travel; 3) a way of building your network of clients; 4) the chance to make your car payments; or 5) making the day more pleasant for a stranger.

33. **Re-frame your work into more motivating language.** For example, you might say, "I'm cleaning up the environment," instead of saying, "I have to clean the garage." Or, instead of "trying to come up with some new advertising ideas," declare "I'm building a million-dollar marketing plan." After all, your attitude *might very well* make your ideas become worth a million.

34. **Use your dreams—literally.** Right before you go to sleep, think about a goal of yours. Get a strong mental image of it in your mind and do this night after night until your dreams are about the task you want. You may dream symbolically, so be ready and receptive for ideas, connections, and solutions that come to you during the night. In the morning, get up slowly and try to stay in that drowsy dream state for as long as possible so that you can best recall your dreams. Try to figure out what they are telling you, and act on those messages.

35. Figure out all the reasons *why* you want to reach your goals. Come up with every personal benefit you can possibly imagine, like joy, self-confidence, peace of mind. Write all of them down and read the resulting list daily. Re-live the benefits as often as needed to ignite the fires within you.

36. **Make *more* progress by doing *less*.** Maybe you are doing something that is taking up a lot of valuable time—time that you could and should be investing elsewhere. Work toward eliminating the "C" priorities from your life. Delegate, simplify, or eliminate them as soon as possible.

37. **Avoid negative labeling.**
Don't say, "The job is so frustrating and much harder than I thought it'd be." Instead, distance that frustration and objectively say, "So far, it's taken me forty-five minutes. That's too long, so I'll need to re-think my strategies." And then, do so. This in and of itself is a much more concrete and effective strategy.

38. Get a quick energy boost.

Eat a piece of fruit (bananas, apples, pears, peaches, melons), or have a glass of natural fruit juice or a high fiber energy bar. Research has proven that "nibbling" at many points throughout the day is much more effective in delivering constant energy than three heavy meals a day.

39. **Embrace every success along the path.** At every step of the way, attribute any success to yourself. A friend of mine claims, "If a miracle takes place within five miles of me, I take credit for it." That's a bit arrogant—but you get the idea. By the way, accept blame for the failures, too. (Consider these as the feedback you needed to make adjustments in your strategy.)

40. **Start with the small things.** Motivate yourself to do minor things like taking out the trash, gardening, eating one less dessert, or giving yourself just one extra compliment a day. This will build a success mindset that can then carry over to the big stuff.

41. **Threaten yourself with loss if you don't succeed.** Write out a check to the most obnoxious group you can think of—a group whose ideology you strongly oppose—and then give that check to your spouse or best friend. Then, if you don't complete your goal, the person who holds your check must send it to that group.

42. **Make your own "fortune cookies."** Write down positive words of encouragement—such as "Today could be the day you do the impossible"—and fold up the piece of paper. Plant it in your wallet, purse, pair of jeans, or suit pocket. Later, when you rediscover it, it'll provide you with a nice boost.

43. **Put your "down-time" to better use.** Many authors are part of "The Five-Mile-High Writer's Club": Using laptop computers, they write entire books solely on airplane trips—a period of time during which they used to do nothing of import. You can do this too: start with something small and finish it during those moments of time you consider dead or down-time. After all, every waterfall starts with a single drop of water.

44. **Motivate others to do something *they* want to do.** Ask them to describe to you the most effective way of encouraging them. If they'll let you, become their "coach." Or, consider community service roles like being a scout leader, a club sponsor, a theater director, or a sports coach. Motivating others will give you an enthusiasm and drive that will become a part of your own life.

45. **Take a ten-minute "power-nap" every day.** First, set an alarm, or arrange to have a friend waken you at the appropriate time. Second, place a notepad and pen nearby. Now, close your eyes and put your feet up. Relax each of your legs, arms, and shoulders, letting gravity settle them into the most comfortable position. Take in slow, deep breaths. Hold them for the count of five, then exhale slowly. If thoughts enter your mind, gently let them go. If they seem important, write them down, just so that you can get them off your mind. If you actually fall asleep, that's fine. If you stay awake, that's fine, too. After ten minutes, you'll feel revived and ready to go.

46. **Have your mind be your personal movie theater.** Think of the most motivating scene you can from one of your favorite movies. Then, see and hear it in your mind. Maybe what inspires you is the runners from *Chariots of Fire*, Rocky Balboa running up the steps to work out to the background theme song of *Rocky*, or a scene from the *Indiana Jones* or *Star Wars* movies. Once you have decided on the scene, run it over and over again in your mind with the sounds blasting away. That will often inspire you to action.

47. **Employ "mirror talk."** Talk out loud to yourself about what you are doing, as if you could see yourself in a mirror. For example, say, "I am now sitting on the sofa ... I am now getting ready to get up and go mow the lawn ... I am now standing up and moving my feet ... now walking toward the yard ..." This provides so much specific feedback to the brain that it helps keep you focused and on the right track.

48. Hold the mindset, "Possible in the world, possible for me." You may need to change your path to triumph, but as long as you keep this outlook, you've got it made. Walk and sit as if you *own* this attitude, and it is more likely to become real. How? Every habit starts with an action, even if it's just a little one.

49. **Develop a stronger response to the question, "How are you today?"** The usual response is, "Fine, thanks," or "Not bad; how about you?" Since you actually seem to *feel* that way when you answer that way, why not respond more enthusiastically, to see if your response positively influences your disposition? Answer by saying, "Terrific," "Good and only getting better," or "Sensational." By answering in a more positive way, you actually *can* start to feel that way. Try it! (By the way, how *are* you today? Four-star, two thumbs up?!)

50. **Talk to a psychic about your dreams or goals.** (Or you can go to a palm reader, someone who does the I Ching, or a Tarot card reader.) Ask what obstacles may be hindering the attainment of your dreams. Inquire as to the forces at play and the solutions you can use to overcome any impediments. You'll get either a new perspective, a shot of optimism, or renewed hope.

51. **Embark on "the future test."** Sit in a chair, relax, and close your eyes. Think of the task to do. Take yourself far into the future, until you are just past the completion of the task. Ask yourself how you feel about yourself now that you actually have accomplished your task. Now imagine how you'd feel if you *didn't* accomplish your task. Which do you like better? Now go further ahead into the future, and again ask yourself about doing or not doing the task. Now, come back to the present. How do you feel about accomplishing your dream? You should be experiencing an extra surge of adrenaline!

52. **Send your energy in the right direction.** Ask yourself these simple questions about your goal: 1) "What's the worst that can happen? Could I live through that?"; 2) "What's the best that could happen?"; 3) "Will my life or the lives of others be enriched by this experience?"; 4) "What's the fastest, safest, easiest way to do a quality job?"; 5) "If not now, when should I do it?" Or, "What would it take for me to start right now?" Focusing like this begets power.

53. Devise a mock newspaper article on yourself that has you accomplishing your goals. Print it out on your word processor, or write it out by hand neatly if you don't have a printer. Post the fake article where you'll see it the most. Read it and believe in your positive destiny each and every day.

54. **Designate a formal weekly or monthly self-assessment day.** On this day, review a list of your goals. Figure out how you have been doing so far in terms of achieving them, and what changes you need to make to help you become more effective. I've been doing this for years and find that the harsh realities of this kind of feedback can be *very* motivating!

55. **Sharpen your brain with visualization right before you attempt the task.** Take five minutes in which you relax and stimulate the brain to peak performance by creating entertaining mental images. In an Oxford University study, students who did make-believe exercises in fantasy and imagination scored higher in their thinking skills. In other words, visualization aids in precision, speed, and creativity when it comes to problem-solving.

56. Cash in on your success.

Buy a piggy bank or any other fun coin bank. Each time something is done that moves you closer to your goals, drop in a coin. When you have reached your goal, you'll have something (the money) to help you celebrate!

57. Make your work into play.

Tom Sawyer made painting a fence seem like so much fun that Huck Finn was willing to give up almost anything just to do it. No matter what task you have to do, there is a way to make it more fun. To make your task a game, put on your favorite music, get your kids to help, or try to do the whole task before the CD finishes playing. Or, turn it into an exhibition of style, flair, and personal expression. It'll help you immeasurably in enjoying it!

58. Keep those you live with inspired.

What you put out, you'll usually get back. I consider my spouse, Diane, to be my number-one supporter. I never want to take her for granted or take unfair advantage of her support, so I make it a point to give her at least five sincere compliments a day. I don't use them to manipulate or coerce; their purpose is to keep our "mutual admiration and support club" in business.

59. **Use pain to motivate yourself.** You may do things to increase your pleasure, but chances are you are also motivated to avoid pain. So acknowledge the pain you would be in if you failed miserably at your goal. You might be disappointed in yourself, might even feel you had let others down. Examine all the negative consequences the non-completion of your task would have in your life. Just for the moment, work yourself into a negative state. Now, use that pain as a motivator to get you moving. Think about how much you dislike the pain and how much you'd like to get rid of it. Now, go do something positive that will help you to avoid that pain.

60. **Work in the proper lighting.** Many people react negatively to fluorescent lighting; it can cause fatigue, slowed reactions, anxiety, and poor performance. Do your work in outdoor natural lighting or under indoor incandescent lighting. Research shows that workers have greater absenteeism and feel greater depression when exposed to fluorescent lighting rather than natural lighting. In the winter, use skylights, if you can, for optimal performance.

61. **Acknowledge your successes.** Make a list, on paper or mentally, of everything that you accomplished, big or small, in the last day. Then, do this for the last week. You'll come to realize you are a very motivated person who does hundreds of small things every day; you simply take them for granted. Realizing what a motivated person you already are will encourage you to take on bigger and bigger tasks.

62. **Daydream.** Rehearse the steps to success in your mind before beginning your task. Make mental pictures of them; talk yourself through them. Feel yourself being successful at each stage of your goal. See yourself succeeding with a smile on your face. Remind yourself that you may even need to try many different strategies to succeed, and that there's nothing wrong with that. Now go do the task.

63. **Read motivating biographies and autobiographies of leaders and others who have "made it."** Read about the successes of Winston Churchill, Eleanor Roosevelt, Martin Luther King, Jr., Golda Meir, "Famous Amos," Debbie Fields, Walt Disney, Sir Edmund Hillary, Steven Spielberg, and hundreds of other inspiring humans.

64. Recruit "three wise men" (or women!) for your project. One should be a person who has a strong vested interest in you performing the task—a colleague, friend, or family member. The second should be an expert in the field whom you can rely on for advice or background information. The third should be a person who knows nothing about your project but who would be interested in hearing about it. They'll be like a board of directors and you can pick up a lot of ideas and enthusiasm from them as they listen to you discuss your project. Call on them weekly or have them call you regularly to check on your progress.

65. **Get more fresh air.** Oxygen breeds motivation, but in the winter it's often too cold and in the summer it's often too hot or humid for us to want to be outside. So often we lack fresh oxygen or negative ions (those are the good ones!). It's your responsibility to find a way to get better quality air—the kind that can encourage creativity and motivation. Open a window or use an ionizer to get air that can stimulate your mind.

66. **Use autosuggestion.** That's a fancy phrase for "giving positive messages to yourself." Tell yourself that you *want* to do the task. Call to mind all the positive benefits you will derive from doing it. Remind yourself of how capable you are. Say to yourself how you plan to successfully do the task. Tell yourself that you intend to overcome any potential obstacles. And finally, point out to yourself how good it will feel once you have completed the task. Repeat the above process daily, each morning and each night, before bedtime.

67. **Compile a weekly activity summary sheet.** Total up how many hours you use for working, eating, commuting, grooming, exercising, sleeping, and spending on family, chores, social activities, and hobbies. How many hours do you have left to work on reaching your goal? Often, it is more than you thought. If it's not, it's time to rearrange your priorities!

68. **Keep the brain active, motivated, and alert.** Did you know that by the time you *feel* thirsty, you already are a bit dehydrated? Drink six to ten glasses of water every day. Make the water easy for you to get at, and give yourself some kind of cue so you'll be reminded to drink it. Use a beeping watch, a glass, a written note, a bell, a visible container, or let some outside distraction be the perfect cue.

69. Ask more of yourself.

Whatever your progress, up the ante. Ask yourself to improve the quality, finish within a new time deadline, or produce more than what is expected—anything to get yourself to bring out your very best. To motivate his basketball team, coach Pat Riley asks his players to give more than their "career-best effort." He doesn't want just "a good try," but five percent "better than the best I've ever done." Adding five percent every day, over time, adds up to new results for the team. What five percent will *you* add today?

70. **Write out your specific goal.** Make it in the present time ("I am now . . ."), positive (avoid any negations), and specific ("I am now the proud and joyful owner of a fit, healthy, and slim body.") Read your affirmation aloud *with emotion* every single day until it becomes a reality.

71. **Expect yourself to succeed.** You have a lifetime of experiences and love from which you can grow and learn. Many others have accomplished great things in this life with minimal talents simply because they had a positive attitude, a willingness to learn from mistakes, and because they worked hard. You can do the same or better—especially with *your* talent. Your own expectations make a big difference, so think big, keep your feet on the ground, and plan to succeed.

72. **Pull together a "motivational" costume.** One of the tasks I dislike is cleaning the garage. But something magical happens when I get dressed in my "garage-cleaning" outfit. I wear a plaid flannel shirt, a big belt, blue jeans, a cap, hiking boots, and gloves. Then I feel like this kind of work is what *I'm supposed to do*; I'd feel awkward loafing off or doing anything else. You, too, should create an outfit that automatically sends your brain the message: "Go do it!"

73. **Check for internal conflicts and self-sabotage.** If you don't feel motivated and "driven" to reach your own chosen goals, maybe it's because you have a conflict of values. In reaching your goals, would you actually be giving up something you want to keep? For example, would you lose the approval of your friends if you took a new job? Or would your accomplishment give you something new you don't want? Be certain you *really* want everything that comes with your goals—and that there are no hidden "side" benefits to reward you for *not* reaching your goals.

74. **Order a trophy for yourself.** It should be one that recognizes the successful completion of your project. Have the name of the task and your own name engraved on it. Then tell yourself you can pick up the memento only when you've finished your project. And once you *do* pick up the trophy, keep it out on a shelf where you can see it often.

75. **Select your words carefully.** Use them to stay positive about your ability to get things done. Never, never, *never* say, "I can't," without adding the word "yet." Avoid saying, "It won't work," except when you add the phrase "unless . . ." Never say, "It's hopeless," unless you add, "so far." Never say, "It can't be done," until you add, "by repeating the past." Never say, "It's impossible" unless you add, "up until now."

76. List a number of motivating words, one right after the other. Choose words like faith, persistence, courage, energy, belief, and humor. Put them near your work space, or on a door, bathroom mirror, or refrigerator. Look at them daily for reinforcement.

77. **Find a mentor.** Ask what motivates him or her. Discuss how he or she does it. Internally (generated from within)? Coming from other people, ideas, things, or events? Then apply those ideas to your own life, one at a time. You may discover that one or more of them will work well for you, too.

78. **Get your family behind you.** The more that others know about who you are and what you do, the better they can inspire and support you. Present a "Daily News Bulletin" to your family at dinner that makes them interested and curious about what you do. Soon they'll be eagerly anticipating the outcome. It's amazing what their support can do for you!

79. **Make a fun and silly bet with your partner.** For example, if you do "such and such a task," then it qualifies you for an especially romantic evening that your lover has to create for you. If you fail to complete that task, then you lose the bet and have to do something special for him or her instead.

80. **Turn on some motivating music.** You know the kind that you like best, but my personal favorites are "1812 Overture" by Tchaikovsky, "Triumphal March" of *Aïda* by Verdi, the theme from *Rocky*, and "Jump" from Van Halen or the Pointer Sisters. For you, it could be oldies rock 'n' roll, jazz, a Sousa march, Beethoven, or even something more subdued, like "Brandenburg Concertos" by Bach or "Four Seasons" by Vivaldi. Put together, on one tape, a whole collection of your most personally motivating music and play it whenever you're feeling sluggish.

81. **Make sure that at least one of your best friends is highly motivated in the same way you are.** It's unrealistic to expect all your friends to be pumped-up, go-for-it task-masters. But be sure you have at least one key supporter who can recharge your batteries. Spend some time around that person each week.

82. Ask an *imaginary* expert.
Think of the person, living or dead, who
could do the task you have before you
the best, the fastest, and the easiest.
Now imagine that person is in front of
you right now. What advice would that
person give to you? If you're not sure,
stand in the expert's place. Take on
his or her voice, mannerisms, and posture.
Now speak as if you're that person. Make
up the advice that he or she would
give to you. And then listen to yourself;
you may hear some real gems!

83. **Allow your wildest dreams to energize you.** Write out a list of every dream you want to fulfill in your lifetime. Then put a due date next to each of them. Which would you like to do within twenty years, ten years, five years, or the next twelve months? After you've marked them with a time priority, get started on those that are on the "within the next twelve months" time frame. These are so close that they need immediate action. (Of course, once you've finished with these, proceed on to those that have the next closest due dates.)

84. **Find a "coach."** It could be any friend or relative who is willing to be on your case, nagging you daily with phone calls or other reminders to do *what it is that you said you'd do.* Talk to him or her about your dreams, goals, and plans. Say what you plan to do, how you plan to do it, and by when. Then let him or her have permission to bug you until you reach your goals. Allow them to be a positive "thorn in your side" or pain in the neck until you reach your goals. This works wonders!

85. Think of a symbol, artifact, or object that could represent the completion of your task. For example, a college student might dream about spending time with his best friends at a sporting event. The object would be a ticket stub from a previous game. Post that in front of you and use it as a physical incentive to get your job done sooner.

86. **Get up and stretch.** Ever wonder why dolphins have so much exuberance and energy? With each breath, dolphins exchange up to 90 percent of their lungs' air; humans average only 10 percent. So stand up. Draw your arms up slowly from your sides, like an eagle getting ready to fly. Inhale deeply. Hold in the air for four seconds, and then exhale slowly . . . for up to eight seconds. Repeat three times. Do this activity several times a day—whenever you have the blahs, whenever you want to change your frame of mind, or whenever you just need an invigorating break.

87. **Rehearse how to effectively deal with distractions and negative-thinking people.** NBA coach Pat Riley calls anyone who can influence you negatively "peripheral opponents." Predict what will be said by the naysayers and prepare a comeback in advance. For example, when someone says to you, "You'd never catch ME wasting my time on that," you can offer this planned-out response: "Well, to each his own ... different strokes for different folks." You'll find that their negative attitude won't diminish *your* enthusiasm anymore.

88. **Activate the brain with cross-lateral activities.** Stand up, take in a slow, deep breath, and let it out even more slowly. Begin marching in place, touching the opposite upraised knee with each hand. Then put your hands behind you and touch the opposite upraised heel (left hand behind the back to the right heel, for example). Now stop marching and take another slow, deep breath. Extend your arm out in front of you and make the "thumbs up" gesture. Move your hand in an infinity sign or in an on-its-side figure eight. Do three of these slowly with the left arm, then switch to the other arm. Take in slow, deep breaths and sit down once again. Your brain will be buzzing with energy and motivation.

89. **Eat more "brain food nutrients."** You can get these in fresh fruits, fish, soybean oil, oranges, eggs, peanuts, oysters, liver, bell peppers, broccoli, chicken, cottage cheese, kidney, oats, soybeans, sweet potatoes, brazil nuts, and other kinds of food. They boost concentration and foster optimal mental performance. Carbohydrates often encourage drowsiness, so you should avoid them in your morning and midday meals.

90. **Attend an inspiring church service.** Some ministers or services leave you feeling "heavy" or guilty and burdened. If you find this to be the case, then avoid them in the future. Go only to those that inspire you to be your best and affirm the goodness in you.

91. **Create a personal motivation ritual.** It should be a gesture, a sound, an activity, or a brief "routine" that is your own "psych-up action." It could be as simple as this: Stand up. Extend your hands in front of you, palms up, about two feet apart. In your left hand, pretend you have, symbolically, the task to do. "Feel" its weight. In your right hand, pretend you have all your talent, experience, fire, motivation, resources, and compelling reasons to get the task done. "Feel" the power of all that focused energy. Now, extend your hands even farther apart and bring them together in a big "*clap*" while saying the word "*Yes*" loudly. That simple ritual gets *me* pretty fired up!

92. **Get enough sleep.** It's so tough to be motivated without it. The optimal amount of sleep varies for each person, ranging anywhere from four to nine hours per night. How do you know your optimal sleep? Simple: just experiment! Go with a half-hour less per night for a week if you are doing fine now, and assess the results. Or, if you're constantly tired, go with a half-hour more. After a week, make a decision. Continue experimenting until you find your optimal rest amount. One more thing: if your "optimal" seems to be over ten hours, you may be suffering from depression, CFS (chronic fatigue syndrome), or some other problem, so go see a doctor.

93. **Alternate periods of focus with those of diffusion.** Focused time is intense, concentrated time invested in just one specific task or part of a task. Diffusion means that the attention is diverted to several things at a time. Focus for about twenty to twenty-five minutes at a time, then get up, walk, get water, take an "oxygen break," or do something different for a few minutes. This gives the brain the kind of rest it needs.

94. **Elevate your personal standards of quality.** Whatever you thought was good enough for effort, add ten percent more. Whatever you thought was enough for enthusiasm, double. Whatever you thought was enough for time invested, add thirty minutes. Operate at this higher level for thirty days. If the results are better, keep it up. If not, keep changing what you are doing until you get the results you want.

95. Know your boundaries.

Before you start, ask yourself, "How much am I willing to invest? How much time, emotion, money, pain, or stress is my limit? How much am I willing to endure? What am I willing to give up?" If you have thought through your personal boundaries ahead of time, you can do any task with greater resolve—and you know when to stop, and when to keep going.

96. **Never conquer only a task; *conquer your doubts, too*.**

When Sir Edmund Hillary, the first climber to scale Mt. Everest, succeeded, he said, "It's not the mountain we conquer, but ourselves." Use your obstacles, tasks, and projects as a vehicle for growth. Welcome the challenge as an invitation to grow and become your best self. Motivation is easier when it's thought of as fulfilling your destiny and as an expression of your awakening greatness.

97. Tie your goal into something else that you *know* you'll do. For example, if your goal is to make five new friends this year, and you know that you already do certain things like shopping, traveling, and visiting friends, reach the new goal by making sure that you introduce yourself to someone each month while out shopping. When you travel, go on a group tour that will encourage new contacts. When you go out with friends, ask them to invite some of their friends to join you.

98. **Gain as much control over the project as you can.** Take on, with enthusiasm, not only the requirements of the task, but the *responsibility* of the task. Then enjoy the satisfaction of being the artist, conductor, producer, and director who make it all happen.

99. **Learn and respect your own brain's natural motivational strategies.** If you're like me, you probably lie in bed for a few moments before actually getting up. Think carefully now: After the alarm rings, what is it that gets you to physically rise out of bed? Is it the images you "see" of what you have to do for that day? The mental movies of what will happen if you don't get up? A loud inner voice that compels and yells at you to rise? Just a *feeling* that you get? Usually one of the above will be dominant, and if that's the case, you've uncovered the technique you should use to motivate yourself to do other things. All you have to do is apply the same technique to the task you have at hand.

100. **Allot a certain amount of time for your task.** Sometimes the only reason we get something done by a specific time is because we have imposed an artificial deadline, which can increase our sense of urgency, exert pressure, and establish strongly needed parameters. Once you determine a date, circle it on your calendar and pencil in the goal. Then, moving backwards in terms of dates, pencil in on successive earlier days all the necessary preceding steps which must be taken first. Keep filling in these bite-sized chunks of your project until you have arrived at today on the calendar. Now, what can you do *today* to make your dream happen?

101. **Take a course in an area that you think needs fine-tuning ... or even a major overhaul.** Whether it's a course in leadership, reducing procrastination, or time management, sign up for it, and really commit to the changes in yourself that are needed to be who you want to be. First you need to be who you really are; only then can you achieve and have what it is that you want.

102. Brainstorm your goal.

Get a big piece of paper and some medium-tip felt pens. Write out your goal in the center of the paper using one to three words. Make the words about the size of a tissue box and circle them. Now start brainstorming your goal. Every thought you have about your goal, write it down on a "branch" that connects to the main goal—in much the way the quills stick out of a porcupine. Include positive thoughts, negative ones, new strategies, and past experiences. *Honor and accept all ideas.* For twenty minutes let your mind free-flow; put as many ideas down as you can. You can even do this with a partner to increase the flow of ideas. Then sort them out, selecting the best ideas to motivate yourself.

103. Talk about reaching your goals as if it's a foregone conclusion that you'll do them and do them successfully. Say, "*When* (or *after*) I finish this . . ." instead of "*If* I get this done. . . ." Also say, "Once everyone's happy with the results, then we can . . ." instead of "Hopefully we won't have too many complaints." This not only provides your own brain with invigorating messages, but also sends out positive signals to others about your confidence in the project.

104. Post *the* most motivating question you could ask yourself about reaching your goal somewhere very visible. Make sure you see it and answer it each day. The question I have posted is: "Today is a once-in-a-lifetime opportunity to live this day fully. How can I make the most of it?"

105. Make a *secret* bet with another person who wants to achieve your exact same goal or a very similar one. But it should be one that only *you* know about. When you achieve your goal, tell the other person that he or she served as an inspiration to you, and thank him or her. (Of course, don't point out that they haven't succeeded at *their* task yet!)

106. Make it *your* idea.

When asked to do a job or task which is someone else's idea, find a way to make it your own. Imagine that assigning the task to you was your own idea. Think of what you could get out of it, why the job might be perfect for you, and how you could grow from it. Think of the social or career opportunities it offers, and what it will feel like to do a totally first-rate job. Then, take on the pleasure of doing *your* job *your* way. After all, it's *your* baby now.

107. Give yourself a star.

Remember how first grade teachers motivated their students? They usually made up a wall chart with names, assigned projects, and due dates. When the daily or weekly goals were met, she or he handed out gold stars. The game became to get the most gold stars, whatever it took. It worked like a charm, because keeping track of your successes does miracles for motivation. Now, figure out how to set up a performance chart for yourself—and don't forget to reward yourself with gold stars!

108. **Do what you're doing while you're doing it.** One of the best ways to stay motivated is to stay in the "moment" or the "flow" of the job and to be "fully engaged." That means focus every moment and idea on *exactly* what you're doing at the moment. If you're doing a report, only think about the report. If you're doing yard work, think only about the best way to tackle it. If you're selling to customers, forget about all other worries from the moment that you greet the customer. It not only makes the job go by quicker, but it makes you do better quality work.

109. **Start every day with a "power drink."** All you need is a blender, food, and lots of nerve! Put into the blender: one cup of citrus juice (orange or mango); a chopped-up apple; a banana; a whole lime with the skin still on; a handful of ice cubes; one-fourth cup powdered milk; one-fourth cup wheat germ; and one-fourth cup natural yogurt. Add a couple tablespoons of honey and blend well. Then enjoy the whole one quart experience for breakfast. You'll get one of the most brain-rich, energy-boosting, long-lasting, wildest-tasting drinks *ever*.

110. Use "warm fuzzies."
Here's how: Acknowledge yourself for
coming up with passionate goals.
Congratulate yourself for starting
them. Celebrate your first milestone. Say
"Yes!" when you reach the half-way point.
Acknowledge yourself for *how* you are
doing along the way. Set up something
fun to do when you complete the task.
And if you're uncomfortable performing
all the "rah-rah," ask if someone else
can do it for you.

111.

Put in twice as much effort as you think it'll take to succeed. At the same time, accept that it may go much faster than you ever thought possible. In other words, plan for the worst but accept all miracles—and usually your task will take care of itself.

112. Collect strategies for reaching your goals and pick out the best ones. Ask others for their opinions on how best to reach your goals. You might ask twenty people and get nineteen useless ideas. But all you need is *one* good idea . . . and once you get it, make sure it's one you actually make a commitment to implement.

113. **Make a game out of your goal.** Get a roll of Life Savers, then poke two pencils into a large piece of Styrofoam and hang all the Life Savers on the pencil on the left. Every time you make a specific progress step or reach a stated milestone, transfer a Life Saver to the pencil on the right. When the pencil on the right has all the Life Savers on it, it will signify that you are done with the task. That's when you go out and celebrate!

114. **Keep the entry point easy.** You're more likely to start a task if it's organized in the way in which you're the most comfortable. Do you like hearing about the "big picture" first, or delving into the details? Do you like to start with what's familiar or do you prefer novelty? Do you want to read about it first or to jump in with a "hands-on" application? Do you prefer structured supervision or a loose rein? If you can, set up the task to fit your style. You'll get into it faster and more easily.

115. Carpe diem. Rent a

movie about the importance of living in the "moment" and the concept of "seize the day." Consider *Dead Poets Society* with Robin Williams, *Ground Hog Day* with Bill Murray, or *My Life* with Michael Keaton. Can you think of any others? Rent them, reflect on them, and start anew.

116. **Use positive recollections.** Close your eyes, sit back, and remember an important moment in time that you had. Maybe it was receiving a compliment or an award, or having a longtime dream come true. Put yourself back in that moment; see what you saw, hear what you heard, and feel those feelings again. Allow the whole experience to fill you up and permeate your soul. Then, take those inspiring feelings and apply them toward your new dream.

117. **Visualize the result you desire.** If you want to lose weight, think about seeing yourself in the mirror and feeling proud. Or dream about the compliments you'll receive because of your new look. If your goal involves your career, think of the pride or the material benefits you'll reap from succeeding. Think of the result every single day—in the morning, and in the evening. Make it a quiet obsession. Long for it. Ache for it. And believe in yourself reaching it.

118.

Monitor carefully any outside influences. Choose your television shows and movies thoughtfully and sparingly. Everything in the media makes suggestions to the conscious and subconscious about values and how to live your life. Some of them you may agree with; others you may not. Dilute their effect by choosing wisely from the get-go. Goebbels, Hitler's Nazi minister of information, proved that if you repeat a lie often enough, people will believe it. So make the decision to read only about positives and to only watch those shows that uphold your own values. Your own "wins" in life will follow more easily.

119. **Get support for yourself.** If you can do the task in five minutes with minimal effort, the issue of support is irrelevant. But a sustained project of moderate complexity or uncharted difficulty invites support. Find out *who else* has a vested interest in your success. Would it be your best friend, colleague, spouse, or boss? This is no time to be a struggling victim. *Get the help you need.*

120. **Make a storyboard of your goal.** Disney has used storyboards for decades. At first, they were used only for mapping out the scenes for a cartoon. Then Hollywood began using them for commercials. Now many top companies use them for planning and attaining goals. First, think of the starting point for your task. Next, think of the ending point. If each could be conveyed as a picture, what would it look like? What interim steps would be needed? Now, get out some paper and make rough drawings of those steps. (If you can't draw, scribble. If you can't scribble, cut out pictures from magazines or make them on a computer with clip art.) Then, post them up in your home or office. The effect is very powerful!

121. **Ask powerful questions.** Ask the person who assigned the task (or yourself, if the task was self-assigned), "How has this been done before? What do you realistically expect to happen and by when? How can I make sure that it's done right? Are there any time-saving shortcuts I should know about? Whom can I go to for help? What's the best that could come of this?" The answers will prep you for action.

122. **Take a drive in the country.** If it's warm enough, roll down the windows or, if you can, put the top down. Let the sun and wind clear out your old, limiting thoughts. Put on the music "Papillon" by David Arkenstone or "Explorer" by Billy Barber. Turn the volume up. Think big thoughts. Drive to the music. Stop at a rest stop or park. Write down your thoughts. Drive for a while again. Think about how to carry out those big thoughts. Stop and write down your ideas. Then write out your first step. Drive home and begin right away.

123. **Consider all the angles of your task first.** Can it be planned out on paper, done in a different order, or made simpler through different tools, new resources, or more time? Just about anything can be made easier and more appealing to do if you work smarter, not harder.

124. **Attend a goal-setting or goal-getting workshop.** It might be offered by a local "Learning Annex" organization, Career Track, any service-oriented businesses, or a local university. Participate to the fullest. Come back from the workshop and start in on your project right away, while you're fresh and raring to go.

125. **Make the completion of your task a huge "must."** If you only "want" to do something, your motivation can be either moderate or strong. But if you "must" do it, if you make it something that you absolutely *have to do*, come "heck or high water," life or death, the task will get done sooner and with more intensity. So go invent a massively compelling reason to get your project done.

126. **Adopt a "once-in-a-lifetime attitude."** Make the most of today because today is a *unique day* that will occur *only once* in your lifetime. You'll never again have exactly the same combination of weather, people, opportunities, health, and circumstances. Since you only get one day *like today* for the rest of your life, adopt a sense of sanctity and uniqueness about it. Then psych yourself up to take special advantage of it.

127. **Distance yourself from any negative emotions you have about accomplishing your task.** Simply, gracefully, and calmly notice them, accept them, and then *let them go*. Your emotional attachment to the task may change, but the task remains until it is finished. Emotions, like the weather, *can* exist without being a distraction.

128. **Extract the jewel from your mistakes.** Think of a recent mistake that you made, and pretend that it was a direct gift from God. If so, what was its lesson? We make mistakes because it demonstrates that we still have more learning to do in this lifetime. Take the valuable lesson you have learned from your mistake, and apply its wisdom to successfully reaching your goal.

129. Pick a motivating word for the day—commitment, surprise, passion, curiosity, perfection, enjoyment, support, teamwork. Use that word as a theme for *all* the tasks you have before you. You'll be surprised at how much easier a new perception can make a day's tasks.

130. Get rid of any household signs or coffee cups that are negative. Toss the ones that say, "Life's a bitch, and then you die." Or, "Insanity is hereditary—you get it from your kids." Or "TGIF." Be *careful* about the messages you give your brain. Get mugs that will inspire you each morning. I have cups that say, "Excellence," or, "That's what friends are for."

131. Use OPM—*Other People's Minds*—as a way to fire you up.** Read the most encouraging, inspirational, powerful books that you can. Try *The Ultimate Secrets of Total Self-Confidence* by Anthony; *Seven Habits of Highly Successful People* by Covey; *Unlimited Power* or *Awaken the Giant Within* by Robbins; *Creating Your Future* by James; *Think and Grow Rich* by Hill; *The Sky's the Limit* by Dwyer; *Winning* by Viscott; *Dianetics* by Hubbard; and *The Greatest Salesman in the World* by Mandino. Or subscribe to *Bottom Line Personal* or *Success* magazine.

132. Tap into the tremendous excitement and motivation of children by watching and encountering them in action. Go to a 4-H show to find children who fully put their hearts into their hobbies. Attend a children's play at a school or community center. Go to your local ice rink and watch the youngest skaters practice their hearts out. Watch a little league baseball game or a neighborhood soccer game. The young are often short on skill, but always strong on enthusiasm. You'll find your own youthful enthusiasm is revived once you return to your goal.

133. Call someone that you haven't talked to in a while. After you've talked, tell them you're about to go do a project. Ask them to do you a favor and call you back at the time you think you will be done with it. Tell them you'd just like them to check in on you. This kind of peer pressure can do wonders.

134. **Create personal motivating statements.** Get fifty colored 3" × 5" cards and write out a positive statement on each one, like "Anything is possible," "Reaching goals feels good," or, "I now have the time, energy, support, money, and wisdom to accomplish all my desires." Write these affirmations in big letters using colored pens. Put them in a stack facing you where you will see them every day. Read one daily, then put it in the back of the deck. You now have your own personal page-a-day motivational calendar.

135. Go on a weekend retreat, the type that energizes you the most. For some, it's an isolated cabin in the woods; for others, it's a weekend with lots of people. Which one is best for you? You know the answer. Embark on the retreat you've selected as soon as possible.

136. Rent a movie about an inspirational person. Some of my favorites are *The City of Hope*, *It's a Wonderful Life*, *My Life*, *The Doctor*, *Rain Man*, *Amazing Grace and Chuck*, and *Children of a Lesser God*. What are yours? Even the process of discovery can be motivating.

137. **Avoid negative generalizations about the self.** If you're feeling lazy and don't want to do the task, don't say, "I am a lazy person." It's better to say to yourself, "I'm feeling lazy at the moment." At the Texas Medical Center in Houston, heart patients were tested and then split into two groups. The doctors said to the first group, "You have high blood pressure. Here are the ways you can reduce it." To the second group, they said, "You were hypertensing when we tested you. Here are the ways you can improve your health." The second group perceived their high blood pressure as a temporary condition and as being within their control, and they improved much faster.

138. Contribute your time to a worthy cause on a regular basis. Call your local United Way, or any of the local church or community organizations. Helping others is a great way to get you in touch with your own personal energy.

139. **Experience the work of professionals in every field.** Go to arts and crafts fairs to meet those who have mastered a craft. Visit museums and think about the vision and passion of the artists. Attend concerts and listen to musicians who bring so much pleasure to the world. Go to a professional basketball game, a high school sporting event, or an elementary school play. And if you *really* want to be inspired, go to the Special Olympics. I've never experienced a dry eye there.

140. **Analyze your home and office environment.** Is there a way that it could be better organized for maximum motivation? Does it foster creativity and focus? Is it inspiring? If not, make some changes. To make it more motivational, bring in plants and flowers, play your favorite music, put positive posters on the walls. To make it more organized, make sure your desk and file cabinets are easily accessible, and buy or update your computer if need be. Get the personal organizer you've always been putting off, clean up your workspace, acquire any furniture that will aid you in operating more efficiently. Start simple and change things until you really feel good about your work area. This does *miracles* for morale.

141. **Learn self-discipline through martial arts, bicycling, weight training, swimming, yoga, dance, or running.** Take an introductory class first, to find out what you like to do, and afterward choose what is to be your long-term discipline. Such activities as these help focus the mind and body in a way that can carry over into other activities.

142.

Increase your concentration through frequent emotional releases. Any small, medium, or big loss or upset in your life needs expression because what is stifled will negatively affect other parts of your life. Take the time to grieve, express anger, and share hurt. Until you express these emotions, they remain inside like a cancer, where they consume valuable energy.

143. **Make silly or outrageous bets.** Bet a friend that you'll complete a task by a certain date, or *before* he will, or *better* than he will. The loser buys the other tickets to a local sporting or theatrical event. Or bet a friend that you'll actually do it (versus not do it), and that when you do, she'll take you to a show. Or bet that if you don't complete the project, you'll do something outrageous like enter a "fun-run"; clean out the closet; give a bottle of wine to a competitive co-worker; or wear a wild dress or crazy tie.

144. **Use that organizer you bought.** More well-intentioned people have bought them than actually use them. The key is to actually make them a part of your life. No one can keep everything in their heads these days—unless they live in a cave. Being organized can help you be less stressed and more efficient, focused, and inspired.

145. **Do reverse visualization.** If you find you are not motivated by rewards, go in the other direction. Visualize the task *not* getting done, see people being irritated, hear lots of complaints, and feel your own stress levels rise. Or, imagine someone else doing the job and getting credit for it. That may be exactly what's needed to motivate yourself.

146.

Compile a "wake-up tape" to listen to each morning. Put your goals on it, make up affirmations, and/or give yourself a pep talk. You can add music to it—songs like "59th Street Bridge Song," "High Hopes," "Good Day, Sunshine," and "Beautiful Morning." When that alarm rings each morning, you can choose to listen to either the same old negative daily news or your own positive psych-up tape. I know what *I'd* choose!

147. **Design a "Road Map to Success."** Get an 11″ × 17″ (or larger) piece of paper and some thick colored markers. Make a symbol or drawing of the end goal you have in mind in the lower left-hand corner of the paper. Then go to the top, upper right-hand corner and put some kind of a symbol for the starting line of a race. Then draw the "yellow brick road" that would take you to your heart's desire. Include any resources, obstacles, and allies on each and every brick. Put along the way dated signposts that reflect achieved subgoals. Soon you'll have an exciting and colorful road map on which you can and should travel.

148. Insist on at least five minutes a day of quiet "down-time." Think about who you were that day, what you wanted to do, and what you actually did. Acknowledge yourself for your achievements and forgive yourself for your mistakes. Then plan on a better tomorrow.

149. **Try the unusual.** You may have a different strategy that works for you. Try the unusual. While others may perform better with a "safety net," or a "Plan B," you may get the most energized with NO alternatives. If that's actually true, burn your bridges. Cut off all options. Have no reserves. Become the leader who says, "Damn the torpedoes. Full speed ahead." Or adopt a "Take no prisoners—nuts to surrender!" attitude.

150. Decide on your dream.

Martin Luther King, Jr. said, "I have a dream . . ." and talked about a world where all people were treated as equals. What is the ideal that inspires you? Ending hunger, child abuse, war, pollution, ignorance, or prejudice? Bigger dreams excite you. They may be more of a longshot, but they also have the sizzle to keep you interested. Your "big picture" vision may even be the energy and "super-fuel" you need to make the smaller tasks happen. So, my friend, what's your dream?

151.

Do a mind-calming, stress-reducing "sitting." Sit upright on the floor, with legs folded and crossed, and hands lightly clasped. You should square your shoulders, push your butt out, and suck your stomach in. Or, sit on the front edge of a chair, making sure that your posture is good and your breathing is full and easy. Lower your eyes, and gaze about three feet in front of you with mouth closed. Breathe smooth and deep, inhaling through the nose. Your exhale should be longer than your inhale. Let go of any thoughts that enter your mind. The power of relaxation and focus is marvelous. Now, get started with the new sense of energy and clarity you have achieved.

152. **Identify with a comic strip character who best symbolizes your efforts to reach your goal.** A superhero or a savvy detective are positive role models for self-esteem, competence, and confidence. But Dagwood, Calvin and Hobbes, Hagar, Doonesbury, Cathy, or Snoopy all have their moments too, even if they're simply offering comic relief from the seriousness of the day. Read the comic strip every day, and no matter what happens in it, take that as a positive lesson or horoscope for your day. You can turn any character or comic strip into a philosophical insight if you truly want to.

153. **Pray, visualize, or meditate every day.** Talk to God and give thanks for the blessings in your life. If you are not religious, simply take time to visualize your life, so that you can see what you have to be thankful for. Giving thanks often gives you even more to be thankful about.

154. **Hang up an inspiring photograph of yourself.** If you don't have one, go to a mall or festival where they do make-believe magazine covers. Get a picture of yourself on a mock-up cover of *Time*, *Success*, or *Entrepreneur* magazine. Post it up in your house as inspiration. It sounds corny, but you'd be surprised how many professional athletes and Hollywood celebrities did the same early on in *their* careers.

155. Stay in the best physical shape that you can.

A topnotch body gives you the vitality, health, and energy to accomplish your goals. Walk, bike, swim, run, or work out at least three times a week. Physical energy leads to mental energy. It also builds the self-discipline needed to reach your goals.

156. Draw up a written contract with yourself.

Identify the task, the date you must meet for its completion, the standards of quality you must reach. Review the contract often to ensure that you are on-track.

157. Get away from *problem thinking* and embrace *outcome thinking*. *Problem thinking* is when you ask, "Who caused the problem?" "Why did I get stuck with this?" and "Where did this mess come from?" In short, problem thinking leads to more problems. Instead, use *outcome thinking*, which leads you toward resourceful, creative, positive solution thinking. Instead of the earlier questions, you'll ask: "How can we best solve the existing problem?" "How can I make the best of my time while I'm working on this?" and "What resources do we have to solve this?"

158.

Keep a notepad and pen on a nightstand right next to your bed. Whenever you think of any ideas at night that could help you, use these tools to record them. Many people report getting their best ideas right before falling asleep and right after waking up. Sometimes ideas will come to you even in dreams. Right now, while it's on your mind, go put a pad and pen by your bedside.

159. **Get ruthlessly honest with yourself.** Look into a mirror and ask yourself the question, "Am I being my best self?" Then answer. If the answer is "Yes," then congratulate yourself and smile. If the answer is "No," then ask yourself, "What could I do right now to be my best and successfully reach my goals?" Now go do it!

160. **Create an imaginary opponent whom you can fight and defeat.** At one school where the problem was student apathy, the staff created a giant villain named the "Apathasaurus." It was a six-foot-long stuffed dinosaurlike animal which represented the "problem." The students got excited about having a "villain" to defeat, and with the new enthusiasm, the Apathasaurus had no chance. The students all worked together to solve the problem and apathy in the classroom pretty much became extinct.

161. Set yourself up to succeed by eliminating your expectations about what will or won't happen. Just enjoy and accept whatever *does* happen. And accept whatever happens as the right thing for you at this moment in your life.

162. Call a time-out.

If you are not getting anywhere on the path toward achieving your goal, take a break for an hour, a day, a week, or even a month ... it all depends on your goal. Sometimes energy, creativity, and enthusiasm drop due to stress, overload, or lack of clarity. Sometimes the best idea is to do nothing for a while. Eventually you'll re-approach it with fresh vigor.

163. **Form a special motivators' club with a few other "like minds."** Meet once or twice a month with the sole purpose of having fun and psyching each other up. When you report on progress, have awards like the "Mt. Everest Award" for whoever overcomes the biggest hurdle. Start organizing this club *today*.

164. Make the task into something BIGGER than it actually is. I hosted some Australian school administrators who were visiting American schools. It could have been unmotivating, but we presented it as an international cultural exchange, inviting the media and setting up tours. The event took on much more importance, and the motivation to do it all went up. Could some pomp and circumstance help the accomplishment of *your* task?

165. Designate a particular location as a renewal sanctuary: a special place where you feel creative and inspired to do your best. It might be a bench near an indoor waterfall, a place by a window, a spot overlooking a lake or ocean, or an entrance to a forest. For me, there's something unlimited and refreshing about millions of grains of sand meeting the unbridled power and passion of the ocean breakers.

166. **Take trainings from the best motivators in the field.** Some of the leaders in motivation are Anthony Robbins, Steven Covey, Brian Tracey, Dennis Waitley, Mona Moon, Charlie "Tremendous" Jones, and Zig Ziglar. After the seminar, discuss it with others, and prevent "post-lecture blues" by buying follow-up tapes and books. Keep your energy alive through support networks.

167. Cash in on "favors owed." Use this *only* when you have a big project with high stakes. Chances are there are others for whom you've done a favor in the past. Now, *if* it's appropriate, ask them for help on your project. (You know what is tactful and what isn't.) Ask them to motivate you, to give you ideas, to lend a hand. Will they do it? You'll only know if you ask.

168. **Make a public commitment.** Tell others around you that you are going to get the job done by stating out loud the due date or time; this kind of publicity will work as an incentive to uphold your prediction. If it's a long-term project, say things like, "Only two weeks left and the project will be done." Then, "Only three days left to on-time completion." Then, "Tomorrow, I'll be done." That pressure sure can work!

169. **Motivate yourself with a silly and fun reward.** Avoid any expensive or complicated rewards, and go for those that are the little joys in life: chocolate, an ice cream sundae, a game of golf, an evening with a best friend, watching the sunset, sitting on a mountain top. Sometimes the sillier and less complicated the reward, the easier it is to reach your goal.

170. Keep learning.

Research has shown that the best way for us to "grow" better brains is to engage in *frequent, new, challenging multi-task* learning experiences. Stressful? They can be ... but what satisfaction you'll experience! So remodel a house—one room at a time—plan a friend's wedding, visit a foreign country, or start up a new organization.

171. Keep souvenirs of your success around the home or workplace.

You want to be able to continually see certificates, thank you notes, trophies, and simple gifts. They serve as a reminder that you *do* make a difference and that you have successfully overcome in the past many obstacles on the road to success. I used to tape up rejection letters from those publishers who turned down a manuscript of mine that eventually became a best-seller. They made me even more motivated to succeed. Now I just keep published book covers framed up on the wall.

172. Create "Operation Total Certainty." Get conservative. Reduce your risks and plan for everything that could go wrong. Brainstorm how to solve potential problems. Discuss what cannot be prevented and what can. Have an alternative strategy and backup plan for every measure you implement. Proceed with so much safety, security, and confidence that you feel unstoppable.

173. Have a heart-to-heart talk with a senior citizen or either of your parents. (If your parents are not alive, how about someone over seventy whom you know?) Ask them about what goals they wanted to accomplish in their lives, and which ones they actually did. Inquire as to what motivating forces helped them attain their dreams. Our elders are a gold mine of wisdom. Go mine it.

174. **Every half-hour or so, take a "brain break."** The brain often needs a break (an *active* break, not a TV break), so get up and stretch. Take in some slow deep breaths, climb some stairs, or go for a walk, a jog, or a bike ride. Shoot some baskets, play with your kids, take a shower, go for a swim, run with your dog, or fly a kite. You'll approach your project in a refreshed frame of mind.

175. **Adopt a "crisis mentality."** Pretend you have only a few weeks to live and that you *have* to accomplish your goal so that you'll die a happy person. Or, pretend you have to accomplish your goal or else you'll be beheaded. I often tell myself, "If I had to face a firing squad if I didn't give it a try, I wouldn't procrastinate any longer, would I?" *This works*. The absence of alternatives clears the mind marvelously.

176. **Wear a sweatshirt with a motivating message on it.** It could say something like "Number 1 and getting higher," or "Always in the top 40," or "Simply the best." These shirts are a cheap form of inspiration and affirmation, and the cost is well worth it!

177. **Re-elicit past successes.** Before or during a task, think of a previous success—about how well you did, how it felt, and others' positive reactions to it. "Bathe" in the glow of succeeding, and carry that same feeling and emotion over to the current task at hand.

178. **Constantly make micro-decisions.** I work out at a gym every morning, although I rarely ever feel like working out when I get up. So, first I'll get up *just* to go to the bathroom and get a drink of water. Then I'll say, "I'll just put some gym shorts on." Once those are on, I say, "Now I'll put my socks and shoes on." Of course, now I can say, "Since I'm half dressed, I might as well finish"—so next I'll put on my shirt and grab my gym bag. Then I think, "Now that I've gone through the preparation to be ready, I might as well go ahead and work out." In this way, I never *really* have to make the decision to work out until I'm actually there.

179. **Practice being highly motivated on very simple tasks.** Take out the trash in half the time, sort through your mail in seconds, and clean up the kitchen during the length of a song or commercial. This "warp-drive" mindset energizes you like you wouldn't believe. Now, pick a simple task and "blast" your way through it.

180.

Follow these two rules: #1. *Get started*. #2. *Keep going*. Just put one foot in front of the other. Keep your eyes open and see the goal completed. Keep your ears alert and hear only feedback and positive messages. Keep your heart open and feel the joy of your success. Get started and keep going. It works every time. I promise.

Epilogue

I was heading back to my home one day after a walk. A runaway horse sped past me. No one seemed to recognize the horse, so I cornered it. Since it had a bridle on, and I was feeling adventurous, I hopped on, grabbed hold of the reins, and said, "Giddy-up!"

The horse immediately headed back out toward the main road. I hoped he knew where to go, because *I* sure didn't know what the right direction was. As the horse galloped and then trotted for what seemed like an eternity, I became increasingly concerned. Occasionally he would forget he was on the main road and start to veer off into a field; I would pull on the reins to call his attention back to where he was supposed to be going.

Finally, after several miles, the horse turned sharply into the yard of a farmhouse. Before I could even turn him back onto the main road, he came to an abrupt halt. A farmer yelled out, "Hey, that's my horse! Where'd you find him?" I said, "About four miles back." Then the farmer asked, "Well, how'd you know to come here?" "I didn't," I responded. "The *horse* knew. All I had to do was *keep his attention on the road*."

And so it is with reaching our goals: seize opportunities, harness passion, and keep your attention on the goal (*and* quit horsing around!).

About the Author

Eric Jensen, M.A., is the author of the best-selling *Student Success Secrets*, *You Can Succeed*, *Brain-Based Learning & Teaching*, *SuperTeaching*, *Learning Brain*, and *30 Days to "B"s and "A"s*. He co-founded the nation's most successful accelerated learning program for teens, and co-designed one of the world's largest accelerated learning and teacher training programs. Formerly a classroom teacher, corporate trainer, and university instructor, he currently does trainings and conference speaking worldwide. His topics are motivation, productivity, and learning. Jensen lives in southern California, and can be reached at: P.O. Box 2551, Del Mar, CA 92014, or by fax at (619) 792-2858.